LOST IN THE CIRCLE,
FOUND ON THE LINE

Lost in the Circle, Found on the Line

A Collaborative Journal Experience

Maria C. Wheeler

Lost in the Circle, Found on the Line:
A Collaborative Journal Experience

Copyright © 2020 Maria C. Wheeler

Produced and printed
by Stillwater River Publications.

Visit our website at
www.StillwaterPress.com
for more information.

First Stillwater River Publications Edition

Library of Congress Control Number: 2020917089

ISBN: 978-1-952521-47-8

1 2 3 4 5 6 7 8 9 10

Written & Illustrated by Maria C. Wheeler
Published by Stillwater River Publications,
Pawtucket, RI, USA.

Publisher's Cataloging-In-Publication Data
(Prepared by The Donohue Group, Inc.)

Names: Wheeler, Maria C., 1956- author, illustrator.
Title: Lost in the circle, found on the line :
a collaborative journal experience / Maria C. Wheeler.
Description: First Stillwater River Publications edition. |
Pawtucket, RI, USA : Stillwater River Publications, [2020]
Identifiers: ISBN 9781952521478
Subjects: LCSH: Wheeler, Maria C., 1956---Diaries. |
American poetry. | Art, American. | LCGFT: Diaries.
Classification: LCC PS3623.H442 L67 2020 |
DDC 811/.6--dc23

To my children...
Aaron Paul
Talia Joy
Justin Mark

and

to my man
Gene Brian

You make my world
go round

...and our little life is rounded with a sleep.

Prospero, *The Tempest,*
William Shakespeare (1564–1616), English playwright

To be Honest is to show Effort, to have Integrity, to be Committed with Sacrifice, Tolerance, Devotion, Compassion, Gratitude, and Patience.

CONTENTS

Introduction

PURPOSE: Who are you?

This book is a compilation of decades of writing, drawing, and living a life. Of endless journal entries, bits and bobs of quotes, scraps of design elements all meshed and smushed into this concept: the most important thing any of us can do is to know who we are and where we are going. Our body does not carry us; we carry it which is the basis of self-esteem, motivation, and contentment. We, must talk to ourselves; look inside to see outside and identify those core values imperative to living a fulfilled life. Life gives us chances to develop when we think out loud and tell our stories.... Writing, poetry, and drawing are all vehicles that facilitate an inventory of our authentic self. This is the most precious gift we give to ourselves and ultimately to others: to slow down, to observe, to develop clarity, and live deliberately.

PLAN: Why are you here?

The premise behind the layout recognizes the importance of both art and nature in informing our higher selves. Both disciplines have the capacity to teach and enlighten. The cyclical nature of the seasons as well as the mutually beneficial community aspect of the natural world create patterns which in turn create structure in our lives. When we align ourselves with this premise, we focus on the collective benefits for the world rather than just the self. We are enhanced by nature, and like a garden, we need to be rooted and cultivated. Without maintenance we languish.

Art is also a necessary practice to engage the senses beyond sight; losing ourselves in moments of creativity refreshes our minds. It develops observational skills and exposes us to a different way of communicating and thinking. Our eyes, as circles, begin to see beauty everywhere and we realize

Beauty is its own excuse for being
—Ralph Waldo Emerson (1803–1882),
American Transcendentalist, essayist, and poet

Objects of beauty elevate our sensibilities and qualities necessary for peace. The circle as a symbol of eternity, harmony, unity, and strength plays a large role in teaching us about life. This book illustrates the concept of circle wisdom—realizing we live life in full circle with everything and everyone, connected in some way. We have the ability to circle back to our past in order to evolve, more enlightened, into our future.

PROCESS: How does this work?

Because a blank page can be daunting, this book acts as a guide providing prompts to jumpstart and inspire written and illustrated work. You will be able to customize your own story as the chapters are organized to represent the ten decades and basic core values of life. The purpose is to envision your life in stages, read between the lines to validate the journey and learn lessons through the writing and the art. You will know that every picture tells a story and to create something collaboratively is a beautiful way to honor yourself, for yourself, and the world.

A life well lived is a work of art. Live it. Show the love.

We got one world till it's time to fly,
so its one love till we say good bye,
We got one world, it's enough to share
'Till we're called home, and
we're caught up in the air
One world.
I'll look out for you.
You look out for me,
One world.
Together we can be perfect harmony.

—"One World," Toby McKeehan,
aka Toby Mac (1964–), singer, songwriter

DECADE
1

To be Honest

And above all, watch with glittery eyes the whole world around you because the greatest secrets are always hidden in the most unlikely places. Those who don't believe in magic will never find it.

—Roald Dahl (1916-1990), British novelist

After all, tomorrow is another day.

—*Gone with the Wind,*
Margaret Mitchel (1900-1949), American novelist

To be Honest

has grasped my soul
toying with my mind.
If not for the sweet
delight of surprise
I would gladly,
silently,
fade away.

The ebb and flow of life
playing with my heart

of limitless love

contribute your own words/imagery to the poem on this page

express yourself in art and writing

YEARS (0–10)
The first decade of life reflects honesty, innocence, and authenticity. It is the age of dependency, playfulness, and curiosity. Our hearts and souls are pure and our minds are free of doubt and uncertainty.

We are spirited, amusing, engaging, affectionate, active, endearing, brave, lovable, and happy. We see with our hearts. We stop and stare. It is the Spring of our lives.

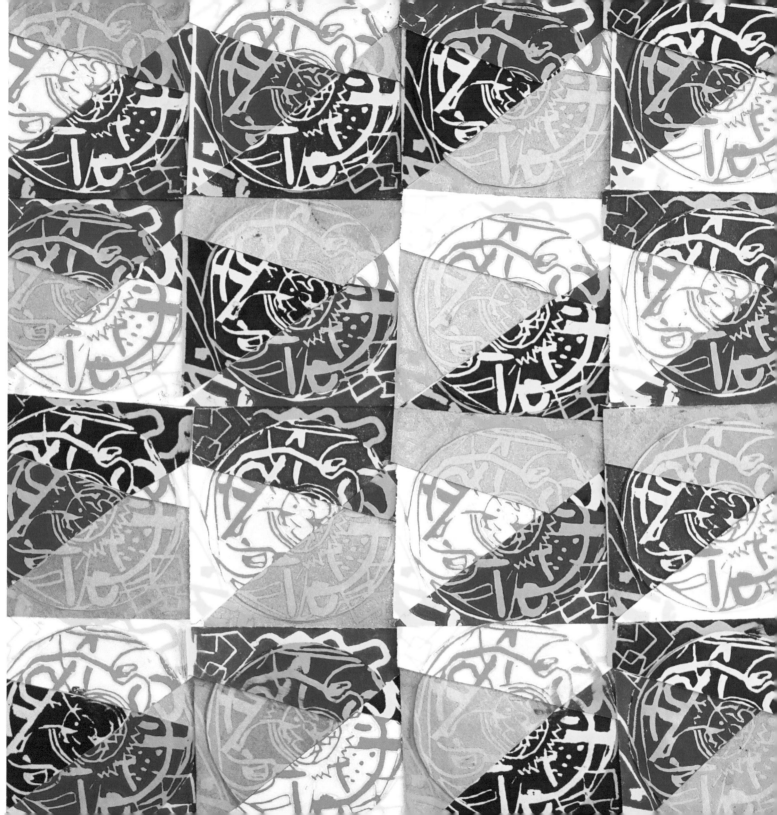

DECADE
2

To show Effort

You have to choose your combinations carefully.
The right choices will enhance the quilt. The wrong
choices will dull the colors; hide their original beauty.
There are no rules you can follow. You have to go
by instinct and you have to be brave.

—*How to Make an American Quilt*,
Whitney Otto (1955–), American author

The most difficult thing is the decision to act.
The rest is merely tenacity.

—Amelia Earhart (1897–1937),
American aviator, pioneer, and author

To show Effort

The world is
as spring arrives
Optimism rides high
Choruses of birds
drab yet melodious
flashy and gravelly voiced
feign courage in the
Season
of
Hope.

teeming with life,
under leaden skies.
on the windless days.

Years (10-20)

The second decade of life reflects earnest activity and conscientiousness. We experience rapid growth and the development of logical thinking. We experiment, are curious, find ways to express creativity, are spirited, sociable, boundless, eager, idealistic, unwavering, optimistic, headstrong, fiery, outrageous vibrant, charismatic, vivacious, bold and energetic. It is the Spring of our lives.

DECADE
3

To have Integrity

The ordinary acts we practice every day at home are of more importance to the soul than their simplicity might suggest.

—Thomas Moore (1779–1852), Irish poet

Only when one is connected to one's own core is one connected to others.... And for me, the core, the inner spring can best be refound through solitude.

—Anne Morrow Lindbergh (1906–2001),
American author, aviator, and wife of Charles Lindbergh

To have Integrity

to the Earth's pulse
with close attention
to the explosions of
fiery reds, mellow ochres
and verdant greens
splashed heavily,
heavenly
scented.
Tenderly ushering in
Spring.

Like nature we respond
and pay homage to days without endings

express yourself in art and writing

Years (20-30)
The third decade of life is the age of independence. It reflects trustworthiness, respectfulness, openmindedness, enterprising risk taking, passionate endeavors, determination, discoveries, adventures, diligence, spontaneity,

exuberance, courageousness, industriousness, ambition, optimism, energy, and resourcefulness. It is the Spring into Summer of our lives.

DECADE
4

To be Committed

The world exists through our senses before existing in our minds and we should strive to preserve the creative faculties of seeing, hearing, observing, understanding, touching, caressing, smelling, inhaling, tasting — for yourself, for others, for life itself.

—Etienne Bonnot de Condillac (1714-1780), French philosopher

The only way out is through.

—Robert Frost (1874-1963), American poet

19

To be Committed

as a noun or a verb
Clipping along at a pace
Yet it does not
stand still.
Time flies.
Forever fleeting,
forever
passing us by.

Time
is meaningless....
faster, slower. STOP.

contribute your own words/imagery to the poem on this page

YEARS (30-40)

The fourth decade is considered the prime of life. It is a time of planning for our future, and of personal growth. For learning about the world, dedicating to a cause, becoming productive, vibrant, tough, knowledgeable, determined, enthusiastic, challenged, receptive to ideas, intuitive, aware, thoughtful, spontaneous, confident, stimulating, and responsible, brave, direct, assertive, credible, and enterprising. It is the Summer of our lives.

DECADE
5

Sacrifice

One always dies too soon or too late. And yet one's life is complete at that moment, with a line drawn neatly under it ready for the summing up. You are your life and nothing else.

—Jean Paul Sartre (1905–1980), French philosopher and novelist

Live a good life. Do good work. Make a difference in the world.

—Samuel Langhorne Clemens, aka Mark Twain (1835–1910), American writer and humorist

Sacrifice

Fireflies dancing on air
warmed by relentless rays of the sun
dripping, sweltering, steaming
Ensuing heat ushers in
the sun baked Earth,
to usher out
an eruption
of
temptations
teasing the senses
to life.

tightening its torrid grip

into the fulfillment of summer.

contribute your own words/imagery to the poem on this page

express yourself in art and writing

YEARS (40–50)
The fifth decade of life is considered middle age. It is a time of evaluation of our past and future. It often reflects sacrifice, giving something up for a higher purpose or for success. Hard work, thoughtfulness, being

ambitious, insightful with faithful service to others. Attentiveness, diligence, consistency, reliability, family oriented, resolute, productive and loyal. It is the Summer of our lives.

DECADE
6

Tolerance

Keep on nodding terms with the people we used to be whether one finds them attractive company or not.

—Joan Didion (1934–), American writer

Be faithful in small things because it is in them that your strength lies.

—Mary Teresa Bojaxhiu, aka Mother Theresa (1910–1997),
Catholic nun and missionary

Tolerance

all about what appears
Ripening fruits
on the
vine
Hurry to complete their mission.
Perfuming the air
with fragrance
and the Earth
with the sweetness
of unfinished Business
and
pleasure.

The waiting game is more important.

express yourself in art and writing

YEARS (50-60)

The sixth decade reflects our ability to realistically assess our position in the world, and acknowledge accountability for our actions. It includes respect for the behavior of others. We have compassion and acceptance, reflection, self-assuredness, reliability, loyalty, leadership, ability to motivate and inspire, responsibility and unwavering trustworthiness, success, focus, understanding, industriousness, consistency, earnestness, and insight. It is the Summer into Autumn of our lives.

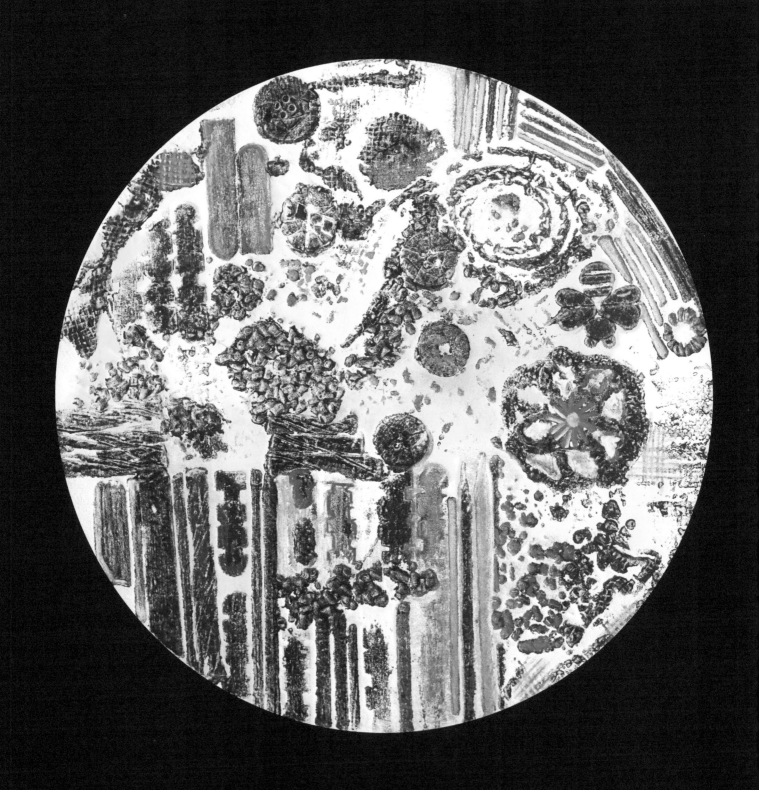

DECADE
7

Devotion

To forget how to dig the earth and tend the soil is to forget ourselves.

—Mahatma Gandhi (1869-1948), Indian lawyer, activist and writer

Where the spirit does not work with the hand there is no art.

—Leonardo DaVinci (1452-1519), Italian polymath and painter

Devotion

So many ways
to
Flying high
ready
to mash our bodies
into one.
A temporary condition
until the inevitable
of sailing
low
the chop
into
the
fog.

travel through life.
was a sign of a crash

one never tires from

Years (60-70)
The seventh decade of life reflects devotion to an enterprise, being dedicated and loyal, discreet, direct, logical, wise, comfortable with ourselves, fair minded with a commitment to justice, respectful of others,

sensible, approachable, insightful, thoughtful, brave, communicative, venturous, calm, honorable, resolute, secure, objective, accomplished, knowledgeable, skillful, and dependable. We are bold, attentive, congenial and helpful. It is the Autumn of our lives.

DECADE
8

Compassion

In spite of illness, in spite of the arch enemy sorrow, one can remain alive long past the usual date of disintegration if one is unafraid of change, insatiable in intellectual curiosity, interested in big things, and happy in small ways.

—Edith Wharton (1862-1937), American novelist and designer

Compassion

In
the blush of the sky
a fading
hazing
burnished glow
scarlet
vermillion and gold
bleach gray
stalks
of grass,
and
woodlands silvery blue.
Colors of the rainbow
dress
the Earth.

the moon looms large on the horizon,

to clutch the daylight, inciting darkness.

contribute your own words/imagery to the poem on this page

Years (70-80)
Mobility is often at the forefront of the eighth decade and years of living reflect compassion as a concern for the suffering of others, a sense of belonging and acceptance, connectedness, faithfulness, honesty,

security, embracing simplicity, being contemplative, deserving, wise, sensible, brave, reserved, dependable, introspective, comfortable, authentic, spiritual, approachable, intuitive, calm, straight forward, conscientious, sentimental, earnest. It is the Autumn of our lives.

DECADE
9

Gratitude

And you, when will you begin the journey
into yourself?

—Rumi (1207–1273), Persian poet

I look back on my life like a good day's work; it
was done and I feel satisfied with it. I was happy
and contented. I knew nothing better and made the
best out of what life offered. And life is what
we make it, always has been, always will be.

—Anna May Robertson Moses, aka Grandma Moses (1860–1961), American folk artist

Gratitude

The uneventful any day.
The squares went blank
where the events went
on,
recorded
Off the grid
off the page,
for none to see.

It happened one day.
Time stopped... on paper.

elsewhere.

YEARS (80-90)

The ninth decade is one of increased dependence yet often with a steadfast manner. To come to terms with the ultimate limitations of aging it reflects gratitude—a quality of being thankful, showing appreciation, and being kind. There is a sense of belonging, caring, experiencing challenges and acceptance, humility, trustworthiness, spirituality, being introspective, admirable, insightful, responsible, fierce, determined, fiery, distinguished, brave, practical, perceptive, loyal, knowledgeable, and brutally honest. We are contemplative, astute, lovable, fervent, distinguished and comforting. It is the Winter of our lives.

DECADE
10

Patience

There is only one road before us, thousands of turns in the way.

—"Only One," James Taylor (1948-),
American song writer and singer

Everything that slows us down and forces patience, everything that sets us back into slow circles of nature is a help. Gardening is an instrument of grace.

—May Sarton (1912-1995), American poet and novelist

Patience

With the clarity of a diamond
sharpen the senses
and submit

The stranglehold of life
relentlessly
slowly
methodically
releases its grip...
fulfills its promise
of
Beauty
in
The End

steely blue skies

shrinking daylight
            into
impending darkness.

YEARS (90-100)
The tenth decade of life is all about tenacity and finding courage and grace to continue living as independently as possible; to realize that aging is fierce. It reflects patience, the capacity of forbearance, the ability to accept and tolerate, to endure, to feel a sense of community and family, to be sensitive, spiritual with a

connection to the higher powers. To have a world view, be contemplative, loyal, practical, dedicated, wise, cautious, brave, worthy, compelling, willful, aware, remarkable, persistent, introspective, uncompromising, tough, wise, steadfast and mortal. It is the Winter springing into our lives.

The End is the Beginning

A tree house, a free house
A secret you and me house,
A high up in the leafy branches
Cozy as can be house
Be sure and wipe your feet house
Is not my kind of house at all
Let's go live in a tree house.

—Theodore Seuss Geisel, aka Dr. Seuss (1904–1991),
American author, illustrator, and poet

I am an outside world kind of girl. A nature loving, tree hugging, barefoot-rather-be girl. When given the choice I cavort in the country. Animals are my charges—from salamanders and turtles to ducks and rabbits—all creatures big and small (except deer, those hoofed-rat devourers of lushness) hold a place in my heart. I studied wildlife ecology and true to Willa Cather's quote (1873–1947, American writer), *I like trees best because they seem more resigned to the way they have to live than other things do.*

My world is wildly surrounded by lots and lots of green and other colors quenching a thirst for growing things. A predisposition to daydream fed a predilection to sketch, illustrate, paint, photograph; Garden design as a profession happily satisfied this obsession for all things beautiful.

I also have a penchant for all things broken: chipped, cracked and otherwise compromised, I see irresistible character through flaws. Most times this served my domicile well; other times not so much.... I've broken a foot while moving into a new home, I've broken a knee while moving into another new home, and now I'm breaking a leg while moving into a new zone of independence. Third time's a charm as it took strong bones to walk away from the trappings of the good life where I played the part of a dangling participle—an adjective unintentionally modifying the wrong noun. I've learned that you can't love someone who plays hide and seek, and I chose a window with a view over many windows without. My world, dangling no more, has settled.

I am grateful to be called mom by three who taught me that **housekeepers** may be important for cleanliness of our lives but **homemakers** are vital for health of our world.

My consternation for the future rests with this quote, paraphrased from John Dickinson, (1732–1808, Founding father of the United States):

Divided we stand, United we fall.

...because ALL things are connected.

In the end, as in the beginning, it is ultimately the simple things that define me and make me happy. Like a day for hawks, with rising thermals of heat lifting spirits and carrying worries away, it is the very atmosphere necessary to jump start life from the throes of inertia. The warm earth under my feet and cool breezes on my skin, the sound of wind through the trees, the salty air, the smell of mushrooms, the riot of color in a garden and soothing hues of the countryside, classic music and smooth jazz, a freshly cooked supper, friends who have withstood the test of time, hugging, always hugging and really feeling love.

–MCW

Artwork Addendum

Front cover: *All Things are Connected* —calligraphy & watercolor
Opening artwork: *Trumpeting Flight* —pencil
1 *Apple Tree Under the Stars* —pastel crayon
2 *Blocked Print Quilt* —paper collage
3 *Two Streaming Fish* —pencil & construction paper
4 *Complementary Blossoms* —colored paper
5 *Dandelion Seed Graphic* —ink & colored pencil
6 *Glass Shard* —watercolor
7 *Earth from Space* —block print
8 *Tear Drop Garden* —pen & ink watercolor
9 *Rainbow in the Sky* —watercolor wash & pencil
10 *Plan View of Dumbarton Oaks* —ink & colored pencil
Closing artwork: *Tundra Swan Starry Night* —ink dots

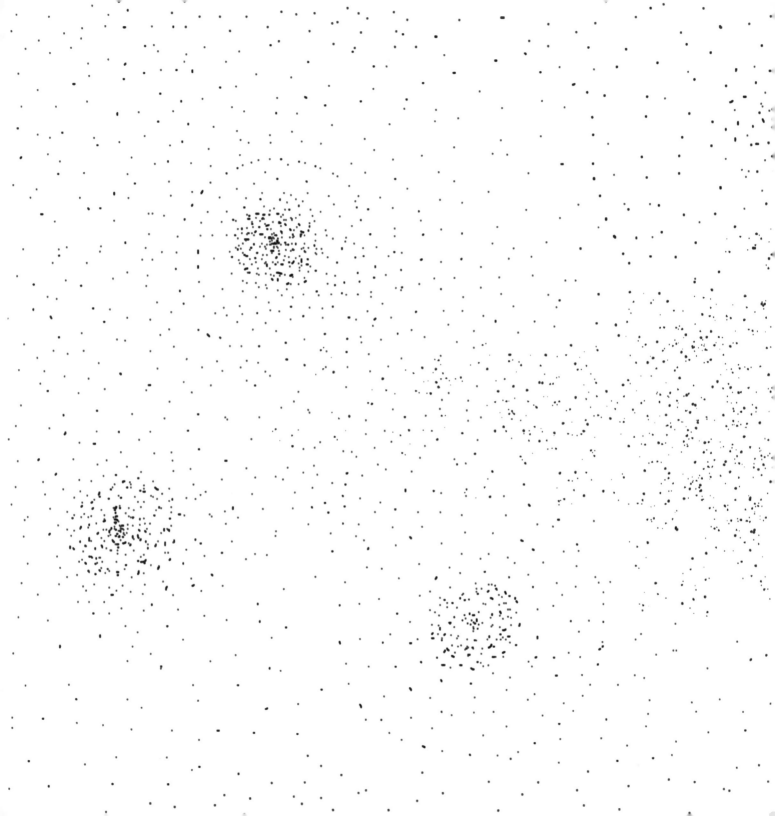

CPSIA information can be obtained
at www.ICGtesting.com
Printed in the USA
BVHW020621270621
609789BV00002B/5